REAL MONSTERS

GIANT SQUID

MYSTERIOUS MONSTER OF THE DEEP

PAIGE V. POLINSKY

Checkerboard
Library

An Imprint of Abdo Publishing
abdopublishing.com

ABDOPUBLISHING.COM

Published by Abdo Publishing, a division of ABDO, PO Box 398166, Minneapolis, Minnesota 55439. Copyright © 2017 by Abdo Consulting Group, Inc. International copyrights reserved in all countries. No part of this book may be reproduced in any form without written permission from the publisher. Checkerboard Library™ is a trademark and logo of Abdo Publishing.

Printed in the United States of America, North Mankato, Minnesota
092016
012017

THIS BOOK CONTAINS
RECYCLED MATERIALS

Design: Christa Schneider, Mighty Media, Inc.
Production: Mighty Media, Inc.
Editor: Rebecca Felix
Cover Photo: Shutterstock Images
Interior Photos: AP Images, p. 23; Getty Images, pp. 6, 17, 21, 25, 27, 29;
iStockphoto, p. 9; Mighty Media, Inc., pp. 7, 19; Shutterstock Images, pp. 4–5, 7,
14–15; Tsunemi Kubodera of the National Science Museum of Japan/AP Images, pp.
11, 13; Wikimedia Commons, p. 10

Publisher's Cataloging-in-Publication Data
Names: Polinsky, Paige V., author.
Title: Giant squid : mysterious monster of the deep / by Paige V. Polinsky.
Other titles: Mysterious monster of the deep
Description: Minneapolis, MN : Abdo Publishing, 2017. | Series: Real monsters |
    Includes bibliographical references and index.
Identifiers: LCCN 2016944852 | ISBN 9781680784190 (lib. bdg.) |
    ISBN 9781680797725 (ebook)
Subjects: LCSH: Squids--Juvenile literature.
Classification: DDC 594/.58--dc23
LC record available at http://lccn.loc.gov/2016944852

CONTENTS

The ocean's surface is calm. But two giants battle in the dark depths below. One is a hungry sperm whale. The whale LUNGES and snaps its jaws. Its opponent, a giant squid, wraps its long TENTACLES around the whale. Barbed suckers latch into the whale's skin.

Suddenly, the whale breaks free. It takes another lunge at the squid. But before the whale can bite down, it is blinded by an inky cloud. The squid makes a quick escape. When the water clears, the whale is alone.

CREATURE FEATURE

NAME: Giant squid

NICKNAMES: Kraken, sea monk, the devil fish, the sea-mischief

CLASS: Cephalopod

SIZE: 33 to 43 feet (10 to 13 m) long

WEIGHT: 440 to 2,000 pounds (200 to 900 kg)

COLORATION: Red and white, silver and gold

LIFE SPAN: Five years

MONSTROUS CHARACTERISTICS

> Massive size

> Eyes as large as a human head

> Razor-sharp beak

> Powerful arms

> **Barbed** suckers

ARCTIC OCEAN

PACIFIC OCEAN

ATLANTIC OCEAN

INDIAN OCEAN

SOUTHERN OCEAN

N
W · E
S

MAP KEY

Where Giant Squid Have Been Found

> Range: Unknown. Giant squid bodies have been found in every ocean in the world.

> Diet: Fish, shrimp, other squid (including other giant squid), possibly small whales

FUN FACT

The giant squid's Latin name, *Architeuthis dux*, means "chief squid" or "ruling squid."

BEWARE THE KRAKEN

The giant squid has been found in oceans all over the world. But very little is known about this monster of the deep. The species was discovered in the mid-1850s. But legends of massive, ship-destroying sea monsters date back thousands of years.

In the 1100s, Norwegian texts introduced the kraken. It was described as a beast the size of an island. Stories of the kraken continued for centuries. Fisherman were extra cautious when rowing into the Norwegian Sea. They believed that the sudden appearance of fish meant the monster was nearby.

People told tales of sea-monster sightings around the world into the 1800s. In 1848, a ship's crew off the African coast saw a creature nearly 60 feet (18 m) long. A British newspaper wrote an article about the beast. Readers were fascinated. Some thought the creature was a dinosaur.

Zoologist Japetus Steenstrup had a different idea. In 1857, he studied a large squid beak that had washed ashore in Denmark. Steenstrup

The kraken is one of the only mythical ocean creatures
based on a real animal, the giant squid!

soon received several other body parts from a **stranded** specimen in the
Bahamas. After comparing these parts to the beak, he determined the
kraken was real. But the creature was no monster. It was a giant species
of squid!

Hundreds of giant squid sightings were reported throughout the 1900s. Most involved dead squid or squid body parts floating at sea or washed ashore. But as **technology** improved, so did the discoveries. In 2004, Japanese researchers photographed a live adult giant squid for the first time in history. They found the squid in the Pacific Ocean. It was attacking a bait line about 2,950 feet (900 m) deep.

Two years later, Japanese researchers captured a live female giant squid. In 2012, American researcher Edith Widder shot video **footage** of a giant squid. It was the first video footage of live giant squid in the wild. Widder's video amazed the world. And each giant squid encounter taught people more about these mysterious creatures of the deep.

In 1873, Reverend Moses Harvey of Newfoundland bought a dead giant squid from a sailor. It cost ten dollars. The specimen became the first giant squid ever photographed.

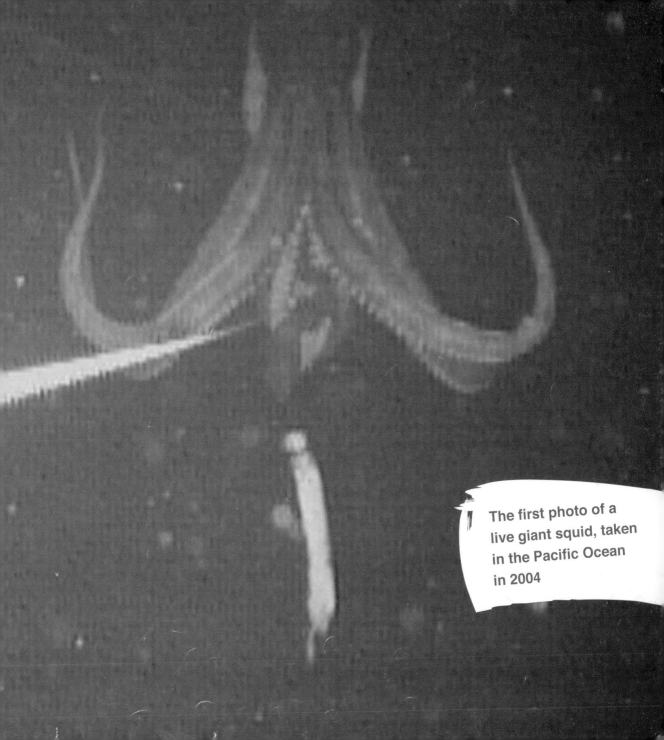

The first photo of a
live giant squid, taken
in the Pacific Ocean
in 2004

A BIG MYSTERY

Scientists have discovered some facts about the giant squid's life cycle. But its deep-sea **habitat** makes it very difficult to research. So scientists study normal squid and giant squid carcasses. They use their findings to make guesses about the giant squid.

Researchers believe that female giant squid only give birth once. But their exact reproductive process remains a mystery. At some point after mating, the mother squid releases millions of fertilized eggs into the water. The tiny eggs float together in a jelly-like clump. Most of the eggs are eaten by predators. The survivors grow into adult giant squid. Adults can be up to 43 feet (13 m) long and 2,000 pounds (900 kg).

FUN FACT

Giant squid eggs are very small. On average, each one is no wider than 0.07 inches (0.2 cm)!

A female giant squid is pulled to the ocean's surface by a research team in Japan.

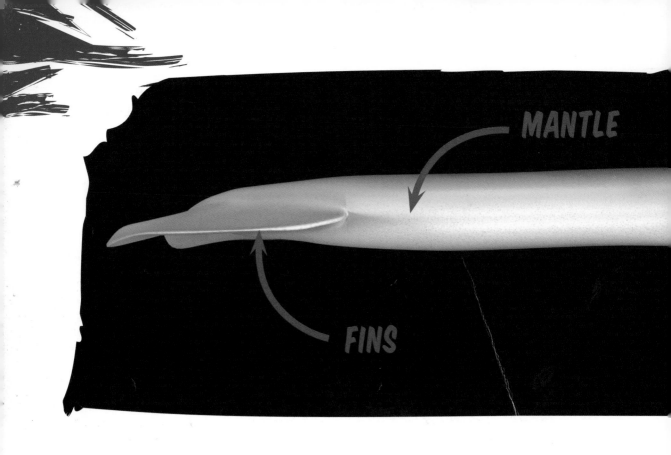

MANTLE

FINS

No one is sure how long giant squid live. However, scientists can make guesses by looking at the squid's relatives. Giant squid belong to a class of animals called **cephalopods**. Octopuses and cuttlefish are cephalopods too. Members of this class usually do not live longer than two years. Researchers are also able to estimate the age of dead giant squid that wash up on shore. To do this, scientists study statoliths.

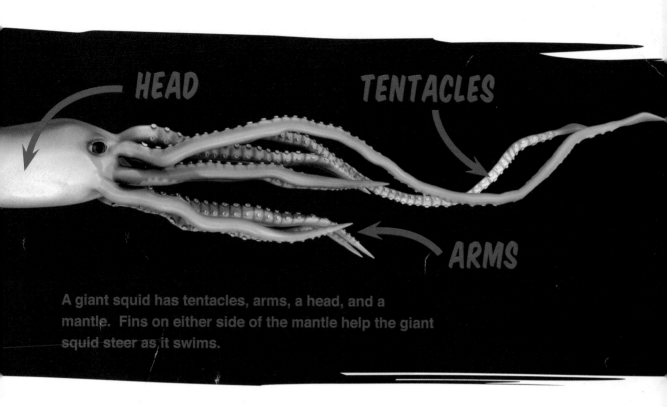

HEAD

TENTACLES

ARMS

A giant squid has tentacles, arms, a head, and a mantle. Fins on either side of the mantle help the giant squid steer as it swims.

Statoliths are small mineral masses in a giant squid's head. Statoliths shift as the squid moves. They help the squid detect changes in orientation when swimming upside down and sideways. Statoliths form growth rings over time. Scientists read these rings to determine a giant squid's age. They study statoliths of many different giant squid. From this research, scientists believe that giant squid only live about five years. That means these squid must grow from eggs to giants incredibly fast!

TENTACLE ATTACK!

Contrary to sailing legend, giant squid do not hunt sailors on ships. Scientists are not sure how these secretive squid hunt. But the giant squid's two long **tentacles** likely play a role. Scientists believe the squid hunts by waiting in one spot and dangling its tentacles downward.

When prey approaches, the squid springs into action. It whips its tentacles at top speed, clutching its prey. Giant squid can capture prey up to 33 feet (10 m) away! The squid passes the meal to its arms, which carry it to its beak.

A giant squid's beak is a powerful eating tool. It is located in the center of the squid's arms. Inside it is a tongue-like organ called the radula. This organ is covered in rows of sharp teeth. It helps cut and grind food.

DONUT BRAIN

The giant squid may be huge, but its brain is tiny! It is shaped like a donut with a hole in the middle. The giant squid's esophagus runs through the hole. This means the giant squid must eat carefully. Otherwise, its food can rub against its brain and cause damage.

BEAK

BARBED SUCKER

The giant squid has a sharp beak. And each of the squid's limbs are lined with hundreds of barbed suckers.

Scientists are also not sure what is on the giant squid's menu. But studying **stranded** giant squid has helped them make guesses. They search the contents of the squids' stomachs for traces of food. However, this food is often partially **digested**. This can make it difficult for scientists to determine what type of food it is.

Scientists' best guesses are that giant squid eat fish, shrimp, and other squid. Evidence suggests giant squid may even be cannibals!

But scientists are not sure if this behavior is common. Some scientists believe the squid may also eat small whales.

We still have much to learn about giant-squid behavior. However, it seems they are solitary creatures. Giant squid are never spotted in groups. So it is thought that they travel alone.

MASSIVE MANNERS

American researcher Edith Widder's ship crew shot live footage of a giant squid in 2012. This footage revealed surprising eating behavior. The crew lowered an octopus as bait. The squid ate the bait in small, delicate bites. It took 23 minutes to finish!

18

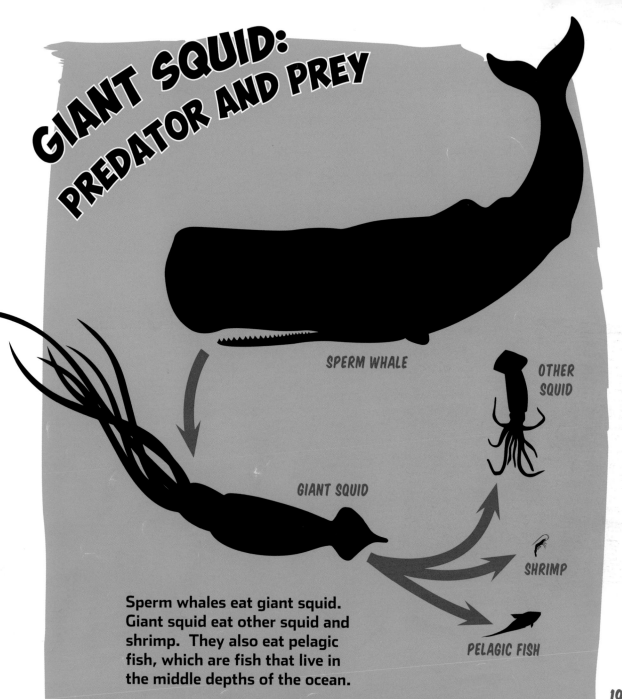

GIANT SQUID: PREDATOR AND PREY

SPERM WHALE

GIANT SQUID

OTHER SQUID

SHRIMP

PELAGIC FISH

Sperm whales eat giant squid.
Giant squid eat other squid and
shrimp. They also eat pelagic
fish, which are fish that live in
the middle depths of the ocean.

19

GENTLE GIANTS?

The giant squid's massive size can be frightening. They can be as long as school buses! But is the giant squid **dangerous** to humans? It is difficult to say. Some experts think these squid may be quite gentle. On December 24, 2012, Japanese diver Akinobu Kimura put this theory to the test. That day a giant squid was spotted in Japan's Toyama Bay. It was 12 feet (3.7 m) long. Kimura decided to swim with it!

Video camera in hand, Kimura swam with the squid back to open water. The creature briefly wrapped its **tentacles** around him. Its sharp suckers hurt his hand. But Kimura was otherwise unharmed. His experience suggests that giant squid might not be as dangerous as once believed.

FUN FACT

Both the giant squid and the colossal squid have the largest eyes of any animal on Earth!

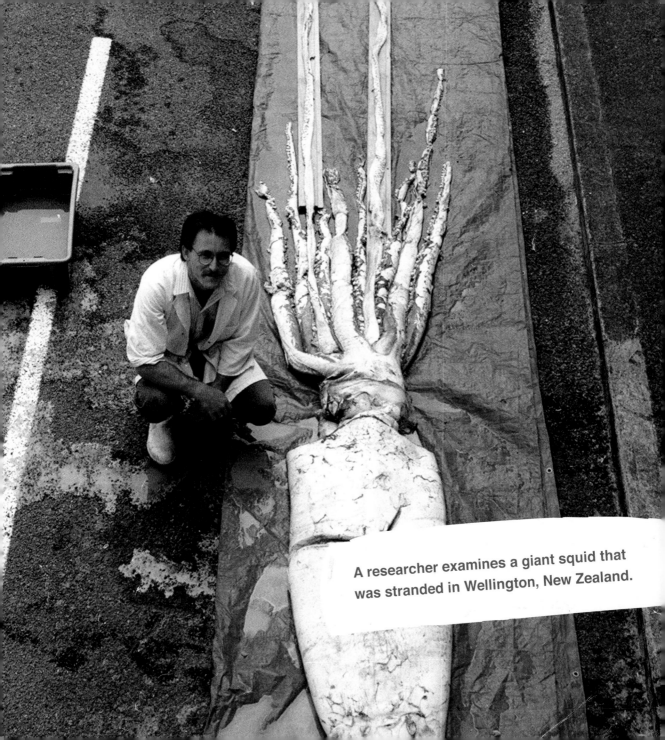

A researcher examines a giant squid that was stranded in Wellington, New Zealand.

DWELLERS OF THE DEEP

Nobody has been able to track the giant squid's exact range. But giant squid carcasses have been found in every ocean. They appear most often along the shores of New Zealand and the Pacific Islands. They are also frequently seen in the North and South Atlantic Oceans. Researchers believe giant squid live all over the world. However, researchers rarely find these creatures in tropical or polar waters.

Giant squid make their homes in the ocean's depths. They often remain between 1,300 and 3,300 feet (400 and 1,000 m) below the surface. This is because giant squid need icy temperatures to survive.

A protein called hemocyanin carries oxygen to the giant squid's blood. This protein does not work well in warmer temperatures. This is why giant squid are not often on the ocean's surface, which is much warmer than its depths. A giant squid trapped in warm water will **suffocate**.

A giant squid's blood requires cold temperatures to function. So, captured squids often die shortly after being brought to the ocean's warm surface.

Scientists study similar squid species and **stranded** giant squid specimens. Their research leads them to believe reaching great depths is easy for the giant squid. The squid **propels** itself forward by pushing water through a cavity in its **mantle**. It does this using a funnel that is located on its head.

The giant squid uses muscles in its mantle to expand the cavity. Water enters the cavity through flaps around the squid's head and fills up the mantle. Then the squid squeezes its mantle muscles to force water out through the funnel. This stream of water gently propels the squid. The squid then uses its fins to steer.

To increase its swimming speed, the giant squid increases the amount of water it draws into its mantle. Pushing this water out more forcefully also increases speed. But using more force can wear the squid out. So, it can only keep up this speed for so long. Giant squid usually reserve bursts of speed for escaping predators, such as sperm whales.

FUN FACT

Giant squid can swim in any direction! They swim up, down, and sideways.

Giant squid have been known to dive up to 3,000 feet (900 m) deep.

DEEP-SEA DANGERS

Giant squid aren't the ocean's only massive marvels. Sperm whales can grow just as big. These large whales hunt giant squid. These two creatures often battle, and scientists believe the whales win most of these fights. Giant squid make up 80 percent of the sperm whale's diet!

But giant squid have some special weapons to help to defend themselves. Dead sperm whales have been found with scars from the squid's powerful suckers. And similar to most **cephalopods**, giant squid have a special skill. When threatened, they release clouds of dark ink. This ink **distracts** predators so the squid can make a quick escape.

Unfortunately, ink can't protect giant squid from all threats. Every day, humans dump waste, including plastics and chemicals, into the world's oceans. This pollution kills the squid's food sources and **contaminates** the water. Yet despite these dangers, giant squid seem to be hardy survivors. Scientists estimate there are millions remaining in the deep sea.

Some ships use large equipment to complete tasks such as undersea oil detection. This equipment often creates traveling sound pulses that can injure or kill giant squid.

DARING TO EXPLORE

It has been nearly 1,000 years since the kraken first became legend. Today, the real-life giant squid is still quite a mystery. Yet we can be certain of its importance to the world. Giant squid are key members of the ocean food chain. They are both predators and prey, helping to keep the ocean's ecosystem in balance.

These creatures also have much to teach us about our planet. Researchers study the **toxins** in giant squid bodies. This helps inform them of deep-sea pollution levels. Giant squid **strandings** have been linked to rising water temperatures. This **demonstrates** the effect of **climate change** on marine life.

Giant squid continue to **intrigue** people around the world. They are a reminder that the sea holds many strange, amazing creatures. But people will never have the chance to appreciate these creatures if their **habitats** are destroyed. It is important we continue to protect the giant squid's

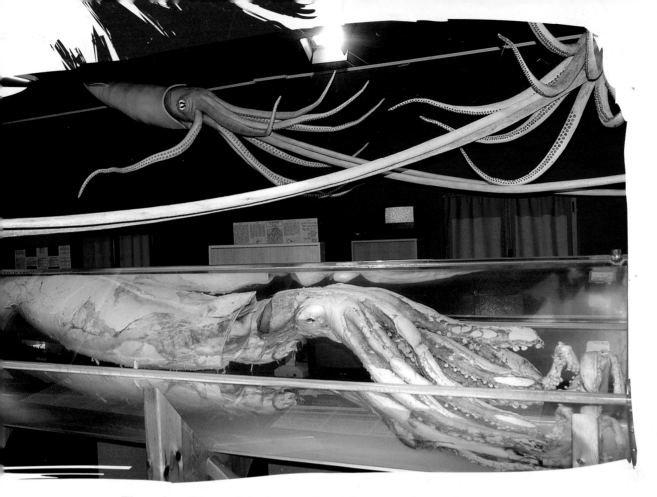

There is still much to learn about the massive and mysterious giant squid.

home as we explore. Ninety-five percent of the ocean remains unexplored. Who knows what other once-mythical sea monsters may be discovered?

GLOSSARY

barbed — having barbs. Barbs are sharp projections that extend backward and prevent easy removal. A fishhook is an example of an object with a barb.

cephalopod — a sea creature that has tentacles attached to its head, such as a squid or octopus.

climate change — a long-term change in Earth's climate, or in that of a region of Earth. It includes changing temperatures, weather patterns, and more. It can result from natural processes or human activities.

contaminate — to make unfit for use by adding something harmful or unpleasant.

dangerous — not safe, and likely to cause harm or injury.

demonstrate — to show or explain, especially by using examples.

digest — to break down food into simpler substances the body can absorb.

distract — to take attention away from something or someone.

esophagus — the tube that carries food from the throat to the stomach.

footage — action recorded on film or videotape.

WEBSITES

To learn more about Real Monsters, visit **booklinks.abdopublishing.com**. These links are routinely monitored and updated to provide the most current information available.

habitat — a place where a living thing is naturally found.

intrigue — to prompt interest and fascination in people.

lunge — to leap or jump forward suddenly.

mantle — an external part of the body that covers a squid's internal organs.

propel — to drive forward or onward by some force.

strand — to wash onto shore.

suffocate — to die from lack of oxygen.

technology — a machine or piece of equipment created using science and engineering, and made to do certain tasks.

tentacle — a long, flexible structure that sticks out of an animal, usually around the head or the mouth. Tentacles are used for feeling or grasping.

toxin — a poisonous substance.

zoologist (zoh-AH-luh-jist) — a scientist who studies animals and their behavior.

INDEX